Manifest Away "ADHD"

Also by The Quantum Shifter

The Truth of Reality
The Biggest Misconceptions About Manifestation
Why Isn't It Here Yet?
Manifest In Steps
Identity Shifting
One Decision Creates a New Reality
Self-Concept Selects Your Reality
It's Just a Reflection
Manifest Faster
Identity Shifting
I AM PERFECT
Embody a Wealth Identity
Mental Diet Mastery
Stop Spiraling While Manifesting
Emotional Mastery
Tell Yourself This When You're Depressed
Manifesting Money 101
Money From Nothing
You Are The Bank
Money Mindset For Single Moms
Your SP Loves You
Manifest A Celebrity
Have The Best Sex of Your Life
Lose Weight The Mental Way
Manifest Away "ADHD"
The Writer Everyone Reads
You Don't Need 3D Proof
Action Is Optional

The Positive Delusion
Cause and Effect Is a Lie
Objective Reality Is a Myth
Revision
Collapse & Command

Manifest Away "ADHD"

How to Drop the Label, Reclaim Your Focus, and Create Without Limits

The Quantum Shifter

Identity Press

Connect with The Quantum Shifter

Website: www.TheQuantumShifter.com

Facebook: www.Facebook.com/TheQuantumShifter

ISBN: 978-1-972432-30-3

Published by Identity Press

These works were written over many years during the author's ongoing study of identity and reality creation.

They are now being published for the first time under the pen name *The Quantum Shifter*.

YOUR REALITY IS WHAT YOU SAY IT IS.

Contents

Before You Continue

This book will make the most sense if you are open to a simple idea: Your reality is not fixed. It is not happening to you. It is reflecting what you assume is true.

If you believe that reality is solid, unchangeable, and determined by circumstances, parts of this book may feel confusing or difficult to accept. And that's okay. You don't need to force yourself to believe anything. You can simply set this book down and return to it later, if and when it feels right.

But if something in you already senses that reality may not be what it seems—if you've noticed patterns that don't quite make logical sense—or if you've experienced moments where things shifted in ways you couldn't explain— then this book will likely feel familiar.

Not because it's teaching you something new, but because it's putting words to something you already know. Read it slowly. Let it land. And most importantly: Don't try to "do" anything. Just see what you notice.

When you stop identifying as someone who struggles to focus, reality stops reflecting struggle.

Introduction: You Don't Have ADHD — You Have Authority

Let's get this straight right from the start: this isn't a book about fixing your brain. It's a book about reclaiming your authorship.

Because what you call *ADHD* is not an incurable disorder – it's a story that's been repeated so many times that reality has no choice but to reflect it back to you. You've been told you can't focus, can't finish, can't stay consistent. But what if those aren't truths? What if they're just loops you've unknowingly stabilized with your words, your assumptions, and your identity?

When you say, "*I have* ADHD," you are not describing your mind – **you're programming it.** Every time you narrate, "*I can't concentrate,*" **you're issuing a command to reality.** The good news is that commands can be changed. And when you stop identifying as someone who struggles to focus, reality stops reflecting struggle.

This book isn't here to argue with medicine or science. It's here to remind you that reality itself is subjective. Every diagnosis, every study, every test result still depends on a story — a frame — a belief system that gives it meaning. Within that framework, things look solid and measurable. Outside it, they're just energy responding to the observer. You are that observer. You are the authority.

You are not broken. You're powerful enough that even your *disempowering stories* come true. That's how potent your mind is.

So this isn't about managing ADHD — it's about mastering identity. It's about realizing that your attention has always obeyed your belief. You've never lacked focus; you've simply been focusing on what doesn't align. The moment you decide otherwise, the so-called symptoms begin to dissolve — not because you forced them to, but because your story changed.

This is how manifestation really works: not by repeating affirmations until you collapse, **but by choosing who you are and letting reality update itself accordingly.**

Throughout this book, I'll show you what happens when you stop making "ADHD" your identity and start choosing focus, peace, and clarity as your default settings. You'll see why scattered thoughts are actually signs of massive creative power, why your so-called distractions are reflections of energy misalignment, and how to flip them back into flow.

The people who told you that your brain is the problem were never wrong — in *their* reality. But you don't live there anymore. You're about to move into a new one — a world where your mind works perfectly for you, your ideas move easily into form, and your reality bends to your decision.

You don't have ADHD. **You have authority.**

Reality never
contradicts identity.
It aligns with it.

Chapter 1

Why Your Labels Are Your Limits

The moment you label yourself, you set the parameters of your reality.

That's how powerful words are. Not because they describe something true, but because they *create* what you'll experience next.

When you say, "I have ADHD," reality doesn't check for medical accuracy. It simply listens and complies. You've declared an identity, and the mirror responds. You start noticing distractions, unfinished projects, forgotten tasks. You don't have those experiences *because* of ADHD – you have them because reality is faithful to your chosen story.

Identity Before Experience

Most people believe their experiences define who they are. "I can't focus, so I must have ADHD." "I'm anxious, so I must be an anxious person." "I struggle with consistency, so I must be undisciplined."

But the truth is reversed. You experience those patterns because you've identified with them first. Identity comes before experience – always.

Once you adopt a label, you unconsciously begin collecting evidence to prove it true. You'll forget the moments of perfect focus, dismiss the days when your mind flowed easily, and highlight the chaos as proof that the label fits. It's not manipulation or denial – it's how the mind stabilizes its chosen reality.

Reality never contradicts identity. It aligns with it.

The Psychology of Narration

What psychologists call "confirmation bias" is just a softer version of reality creation. The mind notices what matches its assumptions and filters out what doesn't.

If you assume "I'm scattered," then every instance of distraction becomes validation. But if you assume "My focus is laser sharp when I decide it is," you'll find evidence for that instead.

Neither version is more "true." One just feels better — and creates more of what you want.

This is why affirmations can feel fake if you're still attached to an old label. You can't say "I'm focused" with conviction if your deeper self still identifies as "someone who struggles to focus." You're trying to overwrite a story without shifting the storyteller.

Identity work is not about lying to yourself. It's about deciding who the narrator is.

The Loop of Limitation

Once a label is accepted, it starts looping. You experience distraction → you label it ADHD → you expect distraction → you get more distraction → and the cycle continues.

This loop can run for decades because the mind prioritizes consistency over freedom. It doesn't care if a story feels terrible — it only cares that the story feels *familiar.*

That's why so many people defend their labels even when they hate them. "I can't help it, it's my ADHD." The loop feels safe because it's predictable. But it's also self-imposed.

You don't break the loop by forcing focus or fighting symptoms. **You break it by dropping the label altogether.**

Freedom Beyond Definition

When you stop defining yourself by limitation, the mind scrambles – at first. It will search for something familiar to hold on to. That's where most people relapse into old identity loops. But if you stay still, reality begins to reorganize around your neutrality.

The moment you stop saying, "I have ADHD," you open space for a new identity to form – not instantly, but naturally. Your energy stops reinforcing the old story and begins seeking alignment with something better.

You might notice bursts of clarity, calm, and ease that seem to come from nowhere. They're not random. They're reflections of your new self-concept starting to stabilize.

Your New Command

Try this simple shift: Instead of "I have ADHD," say, "I have authority over my mind."

Instead of "My brain doesn't focus," say, "My focus goes where I say it goes."

Every word you use is a declaration. Every declaration builds a world.

You are not here to manage a disorder. You are here to master reality through identity.

And that begins with this realization: Labels don't describe you. They limit you.

The moment you stop labeling yourself as broken, distracted, or disordered, you stop creating proof that you are.

Because reality can only ever mirror who you say you are — nothing more, nothing less.

Reality doesn’t argue — it mirrors. It organizes your experiences to match what you believe is true about yourself.

Chapter 2

The Creation of "ADHD" in Your Reality

"ADHD" isn't something that happens to you. It's something that happens *through* you – when attention, energy, and narrative combine into a single identity loop.

Before anyone told you what ADHD was, you simply noticed how your mind worked. You might have day-dreamed often, gotten bored quickly, or moved from idea to idea faster than others. None of that was "wrong." It just *was*. It was neutral.

Then someone, somewhere, attached meaning to it. "You can't focus." "You're easily distracted." "You might have ADHD."

And just like that, the seed of limitation was planted.

How a Label Becomes a Lens

Every label is a lens. The moment you accept one, you stop seeing the world as it is and start seeing it through the filter of that definition.

Before the label, you may have had moments of deep focus and creativity that felt natural. After the label, those moments became "exceptions."

Instead of noticing, "*I'm incredibly focused when I love what I'm doing*," the story becomes, "*I can focus only sometimes because I have* ADHD."

The difference is everything.

Reality doesn't argue — it mirrors. It organizes your experiences to match what you believe is true about yourself. The moment you accepted "I have ADHD," **your world began reflecting it back:** unfinished tasks, restlessness, procrastination, forgetfulness.

You didn't manifest ADHD as punishment. **You manifested it because you believed it was your truth.**

The Power of Agreement

Nothing in your reality can exist without your agreement. Not a label. Not a limitation. Not even a diagnosis.

When you agree that something describes you, you give it power. When you withdraw agreement, the illusion dissolves.

This is not denial – it's sovereignty. You are the authority of your world.

So when you stop saying, "I have ADHD," you're not rejecting science – you're reclaiming authorship. You're saying, "*In my reality, I decide how my mind works.*"

And when you claim that, reality obeys.

The Identity Behind the Symptoms

People think "ADHD" explains why they can't focus. But it's actually the other way around. The belief that you can't focus produces the evidence that you can't.

Once that belief solidifies, it starts generating consistent experiences that seem to confirm it. It's not that your mind is broken – it's that your story is powerful.

You have always had the ability to focus – but only on what resonates. Your mind resists what feels forced. It wanders from anything that contradicts your authentic energy.

That's not dysfunction. That's guidance.

Your mind is not against you. It's simply showing you where your alignment isn't.

How Society Rewards the Wrong Kind of Attention

The world rewards conformity. It praises people who can focus on what they *don't* care about for long stretches of time.

But what if you're not meant to be that person?What if your quick mind, your sensitivity, your constant stream of ideas – what if those are indicators of high creative power, not disorder?

Most people call it distraction because they can't imagine thought operating faster than their own. But creativity doesn't move linearly. It jumps. It weaves. It connects invisible dots.

What you call ADHD might just be advanced pattern-recognition – the ability to see multiple threads at once.

Rewriting the Origin Story

If you were to rewrite your ADHD story, what would it sound like?

Maybe: "My mind moves fast because I create fast." "I notice everything because my awareness is sharp." "I don't lose focus; I redirect it to what matters most."

See how that feels? You haven't denied your experience – you've reframed it as *power.*

The symptoms don't disappear because you fix them. They dissolve because you've withdrawn the meaning that held them in place.

A Simple Exercise

For the next 24 hours, notice how often you narrate limitation. Each time you start to say, "I can't concentrate," "I forgot again," or "That's my ADHD," pause and rewrite it.

Try: "That thought isn't mine anymore." "I'm choosing focus now." "I remember everything that matters."

This isn't about pretending. It's about practicing new authority.

Every time you shift your narration, you shift your identity. And every time you shift your identity, reality has to respond.

The truth:

ADHD isn't who you are. <u>It's a story</u> you can stop telling.

Once you stop, the mind begins to obey *you* again — naturally, peacefully, perfectly.

Every word you speak — out loud or in your head — is an instruction to reality.

Chapter 3

Narration — You're Saying It Into Existence

Every word you speak – out loud or in your head – is an instruction to reality. You're not describing what's happening. You're *deciding* what happens next.

The people who tell you to "watch your thoughts" are partly right, but they miss the core truth: thoughts alone aren't what create your world – *the story you tell about those thoughts* does.

The Narrator Creates the Film

Imagine your life as a movie. The events are just raw footage – neutral, unedited. It's the narrator's voice-over that turns it into a story.

You could walk into a room and say, "Ugh, I can't think straight – my ADHD is bad today." Or you could walk into the same room and say, "My energy's buzzing. I'm processing a lot of inspiration at once."

Same footage. Different narrator. Different world.

You are never inside the movie; you're writing it.

How Reality Takes You Literally

Reality doesn't analyze context – it takes you literally. If you say, "I'm so forgetful," it mirrors more moments to confirm it. If you say, "I remember what matters," it reorganizes itself to make that true.

It's not magic – it's mechanics. **Your narration gives structure to formless energy.**

This is why some people never escape their labels. They tell the same story every day: "I can't focus." "I get overwhelmed easily." "I'm just not consistent."

And so reality politely agrees. It says, "Okay," and reflects it back.

If you want to change your experience, you don't need more willpower. **You just need a new story.**

The Habit of Negative Storytelling

You've probably been narrating your current identity for years. Even small phrases like "I'm trying to focus" reinforce struggle."Trying" tells reality you're not yet doing it.

Most people are narrating a movie they no longer want to watch — but they keep hitting "play" because it feels familiar.

Awareness is your reset button. The moment you hear yourself narrating limitation, you can pause, breathe, and pivot:

"I'm done telling that story." "This scene is shifting." "I'm now the version of me who focuses easily."

You don't need to feel it first. You just need to *say it differently.*

From Narration to Stabilization

When you start narrating your desired identity — "I'm calm, I'm clear, I'm in control of my focus" — reality begins to test your commitment.

Not because it's resisting you, but because it's matching your belief system. It asks, "Do you really mean this?"

That's when old stories reappear, not to punish you, but to give you a chance to respond as the new version of you. The more you respond from your new narration, the faster the old one dissolves.

That's stabilization. That's identity physics in motion.

You're not "training your brain." You're reestablishing authority.

Your Inner Voice Is the Script

If someone recorded your internal dialogue for a day, what kind of story would it tell? Would it sound like a confident director giving instructions?Or would it sound like an overwhelmed actor forgetting their lines?

This is not judgment — it's awareness. You get to rewrite the script any moment you choose.

Here's how:

1. **Observe** the old narration. Don't fight it; just notice it.

2. **Interrupt** it with a neutral statement — "That's not my story anymore."

3. **Replace** it with your chosen command —

"I'm perfectly focused now."

4. **Return** to calm knowing – because it's already true once declared.

Every repetition cements the new identity.

The Law of Narrative Causation

There is no cause and effect. There is only narration and reflection.

When you say, "I can't finish things," that's not the cause of unfinished projects – it's the *announcement* that makes them so. When you say, "I always finish what I start," that narration becomes law.

This is why changing your self-talk doesn't just shift mindset – it shifts *physics*.

Your world runs on your words.

The Truth Beneath the Story

You don't need to control your thoughts. You only need to command your narration.

Thoughts can wander – they're background noise. But narration is choice. It's the conscious author speaking reality into being.

So when you notice yourself saying, “I can’t stay on track,” stop mid-sentence and finish it differently:

“I can’t stay on track... because I’m already there.”

You’ll feel a slight click in your body when you do — a tiny moment of realignment. That’s your proof. Reality just shifted.

Because it always does. It always listens. It always obeys the story you choose.

Your brain doesn't
control you. You
control it.

Chapter 4

Your Brain Doesn't Control You — You Do

The world teaches you to worship your brain – as if it's the command center of your life. You've been told it's responsible for your focus, your habits, your feelings, even your potential.

But here's the truth: Your brain doesn't control you. You control it.

Your brain is not the driver. It's the *hardware.* You – the consciousness – are the operator.

The Brain Is a Mirror, Not a Master

Think of your brain as a beautifully complex reflection system. It mirrors your dominant assumptions and turns them into chemistry, impulses, and sensations.

When you think a thought repeatedly – *I can't focus, I get distracted, I have* ADHD – the brain adjusts itself to fit the story. It wires circuits to reflect the identity you're stabilizing.

That's not malfunction. That's loyalty.

Your brain's only job is to follow orders. If it seems chaotic, it's because you're sending mixed signals. But once you stabilize a single truth — "*My mind obeys me*" — your brain organizes itself around that authority.

This isn't positive thinking. It's mechanical alignment.

You're the Consciousness Operating the Hardware

Consciousness is the electricity. The brain is the computer. The electricity doesn't depend on the computer to exist. It just flows through it — shaping the software, running the programs, lighting up whatever's plugged in.

You could change the hardware tomorrow, and the electricity would still be there. That's you.

When you say, "My brain doesn't cooperate," what you're really saying is, "I've forgotten that I'm the operator."

You are the one giving commands, whether you realize it or not. You're not inside your brain – your brain is inside your field of consciousness.

Why Waiting for the Brain Keeps You Stuck

So many people are waiting for their brain to "work right." They wait for clarity, focus, motivation, or the right chemicals. But the brain isn't the source of clarity – it's the screen projecting it.

When you decide, "I am clear," the screen lights up with matching activity. When you decide, "I'm foggy," the projection shifts to show you that too.

The brain's job is obedience. Yours is decision.

The Science That Accidentally Proves It

Neuroscience tells us that the brain rewires through repetition, emotion, and focus. That's just another way of saying: what you *believe* and *assume* repeatedly becomes your physical reality.

You're not rewiring through "discipline." You're stabilizing a story until it becomes normal.

Even in fMRI scans, the brain doesn't know the difference between imagined experience and physical reality — because to consciousness, they're the same.

So when you say, "My focus is perfect," the brain doesn't argue. It starts building that pattern immediately.

From Victim to Operator

The fastest way to reclaim power over your focus is to stop talking about your brain as if it's separate from you.

Don't say, "My brain won't let me focus." Say, "I decide what I focus on."

Don't say, "My brain is wired this way." Say, "My brain obeys my commands."

Your brain has no free will. It's an instrument. You're the consciousness tuning it.

Once you own that truth, you stop waiting for your "brain chemistry" to change and start watching it obey your declarations.

Practical Reframe

Every time you catch yourself saying something about your brain – pause. Replace it with a statement that reestablishes authority:

- "I am the one thinking these thoughts."
- "I direct the signal; my brain receives it."
- "My focus doesn't come from neurons. It comes from decision."

You'll notice the shift immediately – calmness, clarity, a sense of internal alignment. That's what real neuroplasticity feels like: the brain reorganizing to match your knowing.

The Truth of Identity Physics

In *Identity Physics*, consciousness creates the pattern first; the brain follows. That's why trying to "heal your brain" before changing your identity doesn't work. The hardware doesn't rewrite the software – the software (your consciousness) tells the hardware what to do.

Once you understand this, you stop trying to fix biology and start commanding reality.

You'll never again say, "My brain won't cooperate." You'll say, "My brain is my servant. My consciousness is the command."

And the moment you do – it is.

There's no disorder —
just a story that says
your attention can't
obey you.

Chapter 5
FOCUS IS IDENTITY, NOT DISORDER

Focus isn't a skill. It's not a chemical balance. It's not something you "have" or "lack."

Focus is identity.

You focus automatically when you are being the version of you who knows what they're about. You lose focus only when you start narrating confusion.

There's no disorder – just a story that says your attention can't obey you.

Focus Is the Natural State of Decision

Look at what happens when you fall in love, start a new project you adore, or find yourself deeply engaged in a show or conversation. You don't "try" to focus – it happens effortlessly.

Why? Because the energy of *decision* aligns everything.

The mind only wanders when identity wavers.

When you decide, "This is what I'm doing," reality lines up. Your thoughts, emotions, and actions follow the command. You're not forcing yourself to focus — you're existing in a state of clarity that makes focus inevitable.

That's not productivity. That's alignment.

The Myth of Chemical Control

Science tries to explain attention through neurotransmitters: dopamine, norepinephrine, serotonin. But those are just the biochemical echoes of consciousness — the physical signature of what you've already decided to experience.

When you stabilize the identity of "*I focus easily*," your brain chemistry reorganizes automatically. You don't need to hack dopamine. You need to stop narrating dysfunction.

Your focus problems don't come from chemical imbalances. Your chemicals are balanced around your focus *beliefs*.

The Trap of Fighting Distraction

The more you fight distraction, the more real it becomes. When you say, "I need to stop getting distracted," you've already declared, "I am someone who gets distracted."

You can't conquer distraction from inside that story.

Instead, rise above it. Declare, "I am focus itself."

When that becomes your default identity, distractions dissolve like background noise. They're still there, but they no longer pull you — because the version of you who's anchored in decision doesn't respond to them.

Focus isn't about narrowing attention; it's about stabilizing self-concept.

Attention Follows Assumption

Everything you notice confirms what you assume. If you assume "I'm easily distracted," your mind scans for proof and finds it. If you assume "My attention naturally flows where it's meant to," your mind stops chasing irrelevant details.

You don't train focus — you declare it.

That declaration instantly reorganizes perception, because perception is an extension of identity.

Your eyes see what your identity believes is relevant. Change the identity, and the visual world itself seems to shift.

That's not placebo. That's creation.

The Ease of Being Focused

When people say, "I can't focus," what they really mean is, "I don't know who I'm being right now."

Lack of focus is always a symptom of self-doubt.

When you're certain of who you are and what you're doing, you don't even notice focus – because it's automatic.

The "disorder" vanishes when identity stabilizes.

That's why meditation, breathwork, and stillness work – not because they fix attention, but because they stop the mind long enough for identity to reassert itself.

You come back to your center and remember: "I am the one choosing what matters."

The Command Identity

If you want focus that never fades, you don't need rituals – you need authority.

Say this often: "I command my attention." "My mind obeys my identity." "I am always centered in clarity."

You'll notice how quickly the old patterns lose power. Your environment starts to match your inner stability. People respond to you differently. Things get done without struggle.

Focus is not a fight – it's a frequency.

When you embody the identity of clarity, the universe matches it automatically.

Practical Shift

Try this simple reframe: Instead of "I'm trying to focus," say, "I'm being focus."

You'll feel the difference instantly. The energy collapses from effort into flow.

This is what mastery feels like – not tension, but total calm. Because you're no longer chasing focus.You are it.

The End of the Disorder Story

The label “disorder” is just another way of saying, “You’re not like everyone else.” But difference is not disorder. It’s individuality.

The world wasn’t built for minds that move this fast — but that doesn’t make them broken. It makes them advanced.

When you own that identity — the one who channels thought like lightning — the story of struggle disappears.

Because what you once called distraction becomes intuition. What you once called restlessness becomes momentum. And what you once called ADHD becomes power.

Focus was never the problem. The story was.

And now, you’re writing a new one.

Decision is the action.

Chapter 6

The Action Trap (Again!)

Through Decision and Energy Alignment — Not Over-Effort

When you forget that focus is identity, you fall back into the oldest illusion there is — the belief that *doing* creates results.

That's the action trap.

It's the same pattern you see everywhere: people forcing themselves to work harder, push longer, prove they're capable — because they don't yet believe they already are.

Why Effort Feels Heavy

Effort feels heavy only when you're acting from contradiction. You're trying to create one identity while embodying another.

When you say, "*I'm going to become more focused,*" you've already declared that you aren't. So every action you take reinforces the gap.

You can't climb out of an identity by digging deeper into it. You shift identities – and the effort dissolves.

Decision Is the Real Movement

Decision *is* the action.

When you decide that you are the version of you who focuses easily, who flows naturally, who does things without struggle – you collapse the gap between wanting and being.

Everything that follows is just expression.

You'll still take steps, send emails, write, plan, organize – but it won't feel like *doing*. It will feel like *being*.

That's the difference between effort and energy alignment.

Why "More Action" Backfires

Most people believe action will prove their worth or fix their inconsistency. But in truth, over-action is the physical symptom of doubt.

It's the nervous system's attempt to find control through motion.

That's why burnout always follows – because the energy behind the action was resistance, not authority.

When you act from identity, you recharge as you move. When you act from insecurity, you drain yourself no matter how much you accomplish.

Aligned Action Is Effortless

Aligned action doesn't require motivation – it's automatic.

The moment you stabilize the thought "*I'm the kind of person who finishes things*," finishing becomes your default.

You're not pushing; you're following momentum.

That's the physics of alignment: identity produces energy, and energy determines movement.

How to Shift in Real Time

When you catch yourself forcing something, pause and ask:

- "Who am I being right now?"
- "Would the version of me who already has this be acting like this?"

Then choose again.

Don't fix the behavior – upgrade the identity. The behavior will take care of itself.

From Force to Flow

When you live from decision, reality moves with you. Things begin to line up – people call back, opportunities appear, and timing clicks. It looks like luck, but it's resonance.

Because energy follows certainty, not struggle. That's why you can't out-work misalignment, but you can *out-decide* it.

Your Command

Try this simple reset:

"My energy, focus, and action are aligned. Everything I do is easy because I've already decided it's done."

Say it until it feels true. Not because you're trying to convince yourself — but because you're re-anchoring your authority.

Once that command stabilizes, the body relaxes. You no longer chase progress — you embody it.

The End of the Effort Era

You were never meant to grind your way to alignment. You were meant to decide your way there.

Action isn't how you *get* things. Action is how your identity expresses that you already *have* them.

When you understand that, over-effort becomes obsolete. You'll stop managing energy and start radiating it.

And that's when everything in your life — work, focus, money, creativity — begins to flow on its own.

Overwhelm, frustration, distraction — these are just indicators that you've slipped into an unstable identity. You're reacting instead of creating.

Chapter 7

Emotional Regulation Is Manifestation

How Overwhelm, Distraction, and Frustration Dissolve When You Stabilize Identity

Most people think manifestation is about thinking the right thoughts or visualizing the right scenes. But manifestation isn't just mental – it's emotional.

Your emotional state is your current identity in motion. When you stabilize emotionally, you stabilize your entire reality. When you regulate your emotions, you regulate what reflects back to you.

That's why emotional regulation *is* manifestation.

The Physics of Peace

Emotion is energy in motion – it's what signals your position in consciousness.

Overwhelm, frustration, distraction – these are just indicators that you've slipped into an unstable identity. You're reacting instead of creating.

The moment you return to calm, you return to authority. Because calm is the frequency of knowing.

It's the vibration of "done."

This is why things click faster when you're relaxed. You're not sending out contradictory commands. Your energy is coherent, and reality can reflect it clearly.

Peace is not passivity. It's precision.

The Connection Between Peace, Power, and Performance

When your identity is regulated, your emotions follow – and your results stabilize.

You can't perform consistently from chaos. You can only perform consistently from *certainty*.

That's why "emotional regulation" is not about suppressing feelings – it's about remembering who you are no matter what arises.

When you hold steady in your chosen identity – "I'm calm, I'm clear, I'm capable" – emotions stop running the show. They become signals, not dictators.

The power that once fueled anxiety becomes momentum. The energy that used to scatter your thoughts becomes clarity.

Your performance improves not because you're trying harder, but because you've stopped fragmenting your energy.

Power is the byproduct of peace.

Overwhelm Is Just Over-Identification

When you feel overwhelmed, it's never because of what's happening. It's because of who you think you are in that moment. You're temporarily identifying as "someone who can't handle this."

Shift the identity – and the emotion dissolves.

Instead of saying, "I'm overwhelmed," say, "I'm the calm center of this experience." The situation doesn't have to change first – your identification does.

That's emotional regulation at the level of mastery: identity-first.

Distraction as Disconnection

Distraction isn't a lack of discipline – it's a lack of alignment. When your energy is fragmented, the mind searches for something to ground it. That's why you reach for your phone, food, or any quick stimulus.

The solution isn't more control – it's reconnection.

Pause. Return to the version of you who's grounded, centered, and in command. Say quietly, "I'm right here. I'm safe. I'm clear."

You'll feel the mental static drop immediately, because your consciousness just reclaimed its seat.

Distraction ends the moment connection returns.

Frustration as Misalignment

Frustration is resistance to what is – a sign that your identity and your current reflection aren't matching yet.

Instead of reacting, notice it as data: "This shows me what I've been assuming."

Then shift. "I decide this experience now aligns with my chosen reality."

You'll feel instant relief, because you've stopped fighting the reflection and started leading it again.

That's what emotional mastery looks like – neutrality with authority.

Simple Resets for Instant Calm

1. **The Breath Reset** – Inhale as you say, "I'm here." Exhale as you say, "It's done." This grounds you in presence and finality at once.

2. **The Statement Reset** – "Everything in my world is responding to me. I stay calm, because I know that's power."

3. **The Touchpoint Reset** – Place your

hand on your chest or heart. Say, "I'm safe. I'm steady. I'm me." This re-establishes the identity physically.

4. **The Perspective Reset** – Ask, "What would the version of me who's already living my ideal reality feel right now?" Then feel it. Even two seconds of that shift recalibrates your emotional field.

5. **The Pause Reset** – Before reacting to anything, take three silent seconds to decide who you're being. That pause alone rewires outcomes.

Identity Is the Regulator

Emotions are not random. They're reflections of who you've decided you are in that moment.

The more stable your identity, the less emotional turbulence you experience.

That's why people who seem calm under pressure aren't born that way – they've simply stabilized the identity of *the calm one.*

And because they've decided it's who they are, their reality can only mirror it back.

Your New Emotional Command

"I don't chase calm – I am calm." "I don't try to stay focused – I am focus." "I don't manage emotions – I lead them."

Say those slowly, like laws, not wishes.

Because they are.

When you stop
resisting your natural
speed and scope,
you'll notice that the
same energy that
once scattered you
now accelerates you.

Chapter 8

You're Not Too Scattered — You're Too Powerful

If you've ever told yourself, "*I can't focus because I'm too scattered,*" stop right there. That story is the exact reason your reality keeps reflecting it.

You're not too scattered. You're too powerful.

Your energy moves fast – faster than most people's minds can track – and when you don't yet recognize that speed as power, it feels chaotic instead of creative.

But chaos is just creativity moving faster than belief.

You're Processing More Than the Average Mind

What you call "distraction" is often just unchanneled perception. You're picking up more information, ideas, and possibilities than others can see.

Your consciousness is operating on multiple frequencies at once. That's not dysfunction — that's multidimensional awareness.

You notice details others miss, feel energies before they shift, and can connect patterns that seem unrelated. That's not lack of focus. That's a high-capacity system trying to run on a limited story.

The solution isn't to slow down — it's to stabilize.

When you stabilize your identity as the one who can handle that level of awareness, the chaos turns into flow.

From Overdrive to Mastery

Imagine an F1 race car trying to drive through a neighborhood. It's not built for that environment — it looks out of control, loud, "too much."

But on a proper track, with the right driver, it's poetry.

That's you.

When you accept that your mind moves at a higher speed, you stop judging it. Judgment fragments energy. Acceptance focuses it.

The moment you stop calling yourself "too much," your reality stops echoing that story. Your sensitivity, intensity, and rapid-fire thoughts stop working against you — and start working for you.

The Physics of Power

Energy never disappears. It just shifts form.

So when your powerful energy is suppressed, it mutates into restlessness, impatience, or self-doubt. But when it's acknowledged and directed, it becomes momentum, creativity, and magnetism.

Power doesn't cause problems. Resistance to power does.

When you stop resisting your natural speed and scope, you'll notice that the same energy that once scattered you now accelerates you.

That's the law of identity physics in motion: the energy obeys the operator.

Focus Is About Direction, Not Limitation

The goal isn't to shrink your attention – it's to *aim* it.

You don't need a smaller focus. You need a stabilized command.

When you decide, "*My energy moves exactly where it's needed*," the excess energy stops bouncing and starts building.

That's how you transform distraction into creation. The current is the same – you just changed the conductor.

From "Too Much" to "Perfectly Tuned"

Every trait you've criticized in yourself – the constant thinking, the overanalyzing, the emotional intensity – are superpowers when seen through the right identity.

Overthinking becomes depth. Restlessness becomes drive. Sensitivity becomes precision.

You were never broken. You were just misinterpreted.

When you stabilize the identity of "*I'm perfectly tuned to my reality*," everything that once overwhelmed you becomes effortless.

You start to notice how your natural rhythm creates synchronicities — ideas connect faster, timing aligns, opportunities unfold before you even plan them.

That's what happens when power stops scattering and starts serving.

Simple Practices to Channel Power

1. **Reframe Every "Too Much."** Each time you catch yourself saying "I'm too [anything]," replace it with "I'm powerful enough to handle this easily." You'll feel the charge flip from chaos to command.

2. **Breathe to Direct Energy.** Fast energy isn't calmed by suppression — it's balanced by grounding. Inhale: "I am here." Exhale: "My energy obeys me."

3. **Give Your Power a Target.** When your energy has nowhere to go, it loops. Each morning, declare one clear focus: "Today, all my energy supports this." Watch how fast things move when the current has direction.

4. **Drop the Comparison Game.** You can't measure a lightning bolt by candlelight. The way you operate will never look "normal," because it's not meant to.

The Calm Within the Power

When you stop trying to slow down your energy and instead align with it, something beautiful happens: you become calm *in motion.*

That's true regulation. Not forcing stillness – but being unshakably stable even while moving at light speed.

Power doesn't need to be controlled. It needs to be *claimed.*

And once you claim it, life gets easier – not because you're doing less, but because you've stopped fighting your own brilliance.

Memory becomes effortless once you decide it’s not a problem.

Chapter 9

You Remember What You Want to Remember — Always

People love to say, "I have such a bad memory," as if memory is a function outside of their control. But memory, like everything else in your reality, obeys your identity.

You don't forget because you're flawed. You forget because you've decided what matters – and what doesn't.

Every moment, your consciousness filters billions of data points and keeps only the ones that reinforce your current story. You remember what's *relevant to your identity*. Nothing more. Nothing less.

That's not failure. That's focus in disguise.

Memory as a Mirror of Identity

When you call yourself forgetful, you're not describing reality – you're programming it.

Each time you say, "I can't remember names," your world mirrors that back. Each time you say, "I always remember what's important," your brain reorganizes to match.

Memory isn't stored in neurons – it's stored in identity. The mind retrieves what the self believes is useful to its story.

If your current identity says, "I'm scattered," then scattered evidence becomes easy to recall. But when your identity says, "I'm sharp and clear," your focus automatically follows.

You always remember who you are being.

The Law of Selective Relevance

The mind is selective by design. You couldn't possibly hold every detail of your life in awareness. So it prioritizes what matches your assumptions.

That's why you can forget where you put your keys but remember a single offhand comment from ten years ago. The comment aligned with an identity – maybe "I'm not enough" or "People don't appreciate me."

Identity determines storage priority.

When you rewrite your identity, your memory patterns change too. Things that used to stick emotionally lose charge. Things that align with your chosen reality start standing out.

It's not about training memory – it's about shifting what your consciousness deems relevant.

The Real Reason You "Forget"

You don't forget because of ADHD or distraction. You forget because you're not emotionally invested in remembering something your higher self deems irrelevant.

The mind is intelligent – it releases what no longer belongs to your narrative.

That's why you can remember details about the things you love effortlessly. Passion is alignment. But when you force yourself to remember things that feel meaningless or out of alignment, the system rejects them.

So instead of fighting that, use it.

Align your identity with what matters, and your memory will follow.

Commanding Recall

You can literally command memory back into alignment through decision.

Say out loud:

“I remember what matters because I decide what matters.” “My mind obeys me. I recall with ease.” “Everything I need to know is available when I need it.”

You’ll feel your body relax when you say it, because you’re re-establishing authority. You’re no longer begging the mind to cooperate – you’re instructing it.

Memory becomes effortless once you decide it’s not a problem.

You’re Not Forgetful – You’re Efficient

Forgetfulness isn’t dysfunction. It’s efficiency. Your consciousness doesn’t waste energy storing irrelevant data.

The only reason it feels like a problem is because you’ve been taught to worship “perfect recall” as proof of intelligence. But intelligence isn’t recall – it’s resonance.

You know what you need to know exactly when you need to know it. That's true focus.

That's living from alignment instead of anxiety.

Simple Practices for Identity-Based Recall

1. **Drop the Label.** Stop calling yourself forgetful, distracted, or absentminded. Those words program your experience. Replace them with: "I remember easily," or "I'm perfectly clear."

2. **Decide What's Relevant.** Before you start any task, consciously tell your mind, "This matters." Watch how your recall sharpens instantly.

3. **Use Anchors of Emotion.** Emotion cements memory. Attach good feelings to things you want to retain — pride, joy, clarity. The mind keeps what it loves.

4. **Let Irrelevance Fade.** When something slips your mind, assume it didn't matter. That belief alone keeps your energy clean and confident.

The Power of Assumed Clarity

Once you stop doubting your mind, it becomes loyal again. You no longer have to "try" to remember. You simply decide what's worth remembering – and it shows up at the exact moment it's needed.

That's not magic. That's alignment.

You remember what your story supports. So if your story is "I'm clear, calm, and capable," that's exactly how your mind will behave.

Because memory doesn't come from neurons. It comes from identity.

And identity always obeys the story you tell.

Reality isn't waiting for you to feel good — it's waiting for you to decide.

Chapter 10

MANIFEST ANYWAY

How to Drop All Resistance and Create Regardless of Mood, Focus, or Brain Chemistry

You don't need the perfect mood to manifest. You don't need clarity, motivation, or even good focus. You only need to remember who you are.

Because manifestation doesn't respond to chemistry. It responds to command.

Creation Doesn't Wait for Conditions

You've been taught to believe that you have to feel aligned, high-vibe, calm, and confident before you can create what you want. But that's just another delay story.

Reality isn't waiting for you to feel good — it's waiting for you to decide.

Mood is weather. Identity is climate.

When you stabilize your climate – your self-concept – every temporary emotion passes through without shaking your world.

So if you're tired, unfocused, distracted, or emotional, that doesn't stop manifestation. It only stops when you *believe* those states have power over you.

Identity Is the Engine, Not Emotion

When you declare, "*I am the one who manifests easily*," reality doesn't check your dopamine levels first. It simply rearranges to match your declaration.

Your identity drives the car. Your emotions are just passengers.

They can talk, complain, or cry – but they don't steer.

That's why people who manifest effortlessly aren't always calm or confident. They've just decided that no temporary feeling has authority over their truth.

They live from identity, not mood.

Living From Identity, Not Labels

Every label tries to define your limits: ADHD, anxiety, overthinker, procrastinator, unmotivated.

But none of those labels can survive when you remember you're consciousness, not chemistry.

You're not a brain trying to get better. You're awareness shaping a brain to reflect your decision.

So instead of saying, "I'm manifesting *despite* my ADHD," say, "I manifest easily because I decide reality."

That's not delusion – it's dominion.

Why Your Authority Is Stronger Than Any Diagnosis

A diagnosis is just an official story. It carries weight only because you agreed to it.

But your agreement is stronger than any authority outside you.

When you say, "*That label no longer applies in my reality*," you're not arguing with science. You're changing physics.

Reality obeys hierarchy — and consciousness outranks biology.

The moment you revoke a label's authority, your energy starts to reorganize. You'll notice more clarity, steadiness, and intuition. It's not because you "healed" something. It's because you stopped declaring yourself sick.

How to Manifest Through Resistance

Resistance isn't a sign to stop. It's proof that your new identity is forming.

When old thoughts surface — *I can't focus, I'm not consistent, I'm too emotional* — see them as echoes of a past version.

You don't need to fix them. You just don't answer them.

Say, "That's not my reality anymore." Then return to your chosen identity.

Resistance dissolves through indifference.

Your Brain Follows, Always

The moment you declare your authority, your body and brain adjust.

Energy flows where identity leads. If you say, "My focus is perfect," your brain begins rewiring for that experience. If you say, "I create easily," your chemistry aligns with ease.

You don't wait for physical evidence to feel powerful. You feel powerful – and physical evidence follows.

That's how manifestation really works.

Practical Commands for Real-Time Manifestation

Use these whenever you feel off, scattered, or disconnected:

- "My energy obeys me."
- "My focus is optional, my authority is absolute."
- "I manifest no matter how I feel."
- "My word creates. Period."
- "Everything I decide becomes true, be-

cause I said so."

Say them like truth, not like affirmations. Because they are truth.

When You Stop Waiting

When you stop waiting for focus, motivation, or the right mindset, you become unstoppable.

You manifest while tired. You manifest while distracted. You manifest while emotional.

Because creation doesn't come from perfection — it comes from decision.

And once you've decided who you are, even resistance has to reflect your authority.

The Final Word

You are not broken. You're not limited. You're not your brain, your diagnosis, or your emotions.

You are consciousness — the source of every reflection you see.

When you live from that truth, you don't need to "overcome" anything. You simply decide, and reality obeys. That's not hope. <u>That's law.</u>

You were never broken. You just believed a story that said you were.

Conclusion: You Were Never Broken

The Mind Was Never the Problem – The Story Was

You were never broken. You just believed a story that said you were.

The mind was never your enemy – it was simply following orders. It mirrored what you assumed was true about yourself.

If you told it you were distracted, it showed you distraction. If you told it you were unfocused, it kept scanning for proof. And the whole time, it was just doing its job – reflecting the story you stabilized.

You didn't fail because you "have ADHD." You didn't fail because you "lack discipline." You only forgot that your word is law.

The Power Was Always Yours

The moment you drop the identity of "someone who struggles," you stop struggling. The moment you stop narrating limitation, limitation stops existing in your reality.

You don't have to earn focus, motivation, or consistency. You just decide you already are those things.

Every story you've ever lived — from the most chaotic to the most peaceful — began as an assumption you accepted as true.

And now, you're writing new ones.

Your Mind Is a Loyal Servant

Your mind was never the problem. It's your most loyal mirror. It reflects exactly what you declare, without judgment or emotion.

The story changes, and the reflection changes.

So when you choose to narrate, "*I'm calm, clear, and in control,*" your mind gets the signal instantly. It stops resisting, because it's not built to argue — it's built to obey.

You are not fixing your brain. You're leading it.

The Return to Authority

Every label, every diagnosis, every old narrative dissolves the moment you decide it has no power.

You are the consciousness behind all of it — the awareness that decides what's real.

And once you remember that, there's nothing left to heal. There's only creation.

The Truth of You

You were never "someone with ADHD." You were always a creator experimenting with focus. You were never "someone who can't finish things." You were always a powerful mind exploring momentum.

You were never broken. You were brilliant — and untrained in your own authority.

Now you know.

The New Story

From this point forward, you don't manage symptoms — you command reality. You don't wait for cooperation — you declare alignment.

You don't "manifest despite" your mind – you manifest *through* it.

And you do it easily. Because you've always been the one in charge. You just forgot for a while.

Now, you remember. And reality remembers with you.

Your power was never in how well your brain behaved. It was always in how clearly you remembered who you are.

Bonus: The "Manifest Anyway" Toolkit

Daily Identity Resets, Mental Diet, and Power Statements for Focus and Calm

This section isn't about "fixing" yourself.I t's about remembering your authority – every single day.

These tools help you stay anchored in the truth that you are consciousness, not chemistry. They're not rituals or techniques. They're reminders that your word is final and reality obeys it.

Use them often. Speak them as law. Let them become the language of your new identity.

Quick Identity Resets

Use these anytime you feel scattered, tired, or distracted. They bring you back to who you actually are – not who you've been conditioned to think you are.

1. **The Neutral Reset** "Nothing's wrong. I'm just returning to my command." (Say this before reacting, so you lead the moment instead of following it.)

2. **The Power Reset** "My energy obeys me. My mind follows my word." (Instantly reclaims authority when thoughts feel out of control.)

3. **The Calm Reset** "I'm the stable center of my reality." (Use this when emotions spike. It collapses chaos immediately.)

4. **The Focus Reset** "My attention goes where I say it goes." (Say it when your mind wanders. Don't try to force focus – command it.)

5. **The Decision Reset** "This is who I am now." (Whenever you catch yourself slipping into the old story, use this to re-anchor your chosen identity.)

Daily Mental Diet for Focus and Calm

Morning:

"My word is law. I decide how my mind feels today." "Everything in my world is calm, clear, and stable because I am."

Throughout the Day:

"My attention serves me." "Everything that matters stays in my awareness." "I lead my mind with peace, not pressure."

Evening:

"I'm proud of how easily I stayed in control today." "I release all leftover noise and return to calm knowing." "My identity is stable. My reality is steady."

Affirmations and Power Statements

These are not "positive thinking" phrases. They're declarations of fact – commands to the mirror of reality.

Repeat them with conviction, or read them quietly until they feel like truth again.

Authority Statements

- "My word creates instantly."
- "My brain reflects my identity – and my identity is power."
- "Labels dissolve in my reality. Only truth remains."

Focus & Clarity Statements

- "My focus is effortless because I've decided it is."
- "I remember what matters automatically."
- "Everything I need to know appears exactly when I need it."

Calm & Emotional Stability Statements

- "Peace is my default setting."
- "My emotions serve my clarity."
- "Calm is not something I chase – it's who I am."

Manifestation Statements

- "I manifest anyway – regardless of mood, energy, or focus."
- "Creation doesn't need conditions. It only needs command."
- "My reality always responds to me."

How to Use the Toolkit

You don't need to schedule or structure this. Use it fluidly throughout your day:

- When your thoughts start racing, pause and reset.
- When you feel pressure, choose calm as identity.
- When doubt appears, remind yourself that you manifest anyway.

Every use is a micro-shift in identity – and those micro-shifts compound fast.

The goal isn't perfection. It's awareness. You'll know it's working when effort disappears and peace becomes your baseline.

Because the truth is simple: Your power was never in how well your brain behaved. It was always in how clearly you remembered who you are.

About The Author

The Quantum Shifter is the pen name of an Ivy-trained psychologist, researcher, and lecturer whose work explores the intersection of identity, consciousness, and reality creation. After completing advanced studies in psychology and spending years teaching and writing at the university level, she shifted her focus toward the deeper question that shaped her life's work:

How does identity create reality — and why does changing the story of who you are change the world you live in?

Her publications draw on decades of private research, academic inquiry, and experiential observation. Known for her clarity, precision, and deeply grounded approach, she writes about identity physics, timeline selection, self-concept, and the mechanics of reality in a way that is both accessible and transformative.

Although her academic background is traditional, her pen name reflects the evolution of her work — a nod to the moment she realized that consciousness itself is the most powerful instrument of change. The name stuck, and readers around the world now associate *The Quantum Shifter* with high-level insight, elegant simplicity, and rapid identity transformation.

She currently lives a quiet, contemplative life dedicated to writing, research, and teaching the principles of identity-based reality creation. Her books serve as distilled explorations of the concepts she has spent decades studying — written for readers who are ready to shift who they are, not just what they want.

www.ingramcontent.com/pod-product-compliance
Lightning Source LLC
Chambersburg PA
CBHW031329230926
51848CB00001B/158

9781972432303